WHAT'S THE BIG IDEA?

The Environment

Nicola Barber

Illustrated by Nick Dewar

Is that what trees used to look like?

Hodder
Children's
Books

a division of Hodder Headline plc

Contents

WHAT'S THE BIG IDEA?

What's the Big Idea? focuses on the hottest issues
and ideas around. In a nationwide survey, we asked
young people like you to tell us which subjects you
find most intriguing, worrying and exciting.
The books in this series tell you what you need to
know about the top-rated topics.

Books available now:
The Mind
Virtual Reality
Women's Rights
The Environment
Animal Rights

Books coming soon:
Religion
Time and the Universe
The Nuclear Question

We would love to hear what you think. If you
would like to make any comments on this book or
suggestions for future titles, please write to us at:

> What's the Big Idea?
> Hodder Children's Books
> 338 Euston Road
> London NW1 3BH

This book is dedicated to Anita.

Text copyright © Nicola Barber 1997

The right of Nicola Barber and Nick Dewar to be identified as the author and illustrator of the Work has been asserted by them in accordance with the Copyright, Designs and Patents Act 1988.

Illustrations copyright © Nick Dewar 1997

Cover illustration by Jake Abrams

Edited by Vic Parker

Typesetting by Joy Mutter

Published by Hodder Children's Books 1997

10 9 8 7 6 5 4 3 2 1

ISBN 0 340 67847 X

A Catalogue record for this book is available from the British Library.

Printed by Cox and Wyman Ltd, Reading, Berkshire

Hodder Children's Books
A division of Hodder Headline plc
338 Euston Road
London NW1 3BH

ENVIRONMENT NEWS – FACT OR FICTION?

We're surrounded by TV and newspaper reports which tell us that we're fighting a losing battle to save our planet. Species are being wiped out every minute and rainforest is being cut down faster than you can blink.

KENDAL GAZETTE

GLOBAL WARMING IS HERE

THERMAL VEST SALES FALL

ZETTE

OAL

TOCK

RUN

OUT

CUMBRIAN HERA

TIME

RUN

OU

OBAN TIMES

FAMINE HITS AFRICA

We're all going to die.

SAVE the TREE STOAT

IRISH TIMES

SMOG BLANKET LONDON

COMMUTERS PRET IT DOES NOT EXIS

DAILY SNOO

PANIC

OII

SPI

But is it really all doom and gloom, or is there another side to the story?

Sensational news will always sell papers and make people watch TV programmes. But the problem with sensation is that the news is simplified, and details are often left out.

WHICH WOULD
YOU BUY?

STAINDROP POST

SKIN CANCER SHOCK BLAMED ON HORROR OZONE HOLE

WRITES DINGLE McWHIT

A HOLE YESTERDAY

CUPAR TRIBUNE

SCIENTISTS NOT ENTIRELY CERTAIN THAT OZONE HOLE CAUSES CANCER

"MAYBE, I DUNNO" claims boffin

In all news about the environment the same
'baddies' reappear over and over again ...

... in fact, PEOPLE generally. It's very easy to
blame these baddies for environmental problems,
but is it entirely their fault?

You may not be such a 'good guy' as you think ...

But do you know WHY the rainforests of Central America have been torn up and burned down?

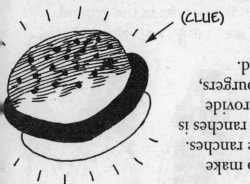

(CLUE)

ANSWER: Mostly to make room for more cattle ranches. The beef from these ranches is sold to the USA to provide cheap meat for beefburgers, hot dogs and pet food.

As you find out more of the story, you will see that there are often many different reasons for a particular environmental problem, and that there are usually no easy answers.

what about sausages — can I eat them?

*See pages 58 to 65 for more about why the rainforests are so important to life on Earth.

11

Every living thing on Earth shapes the environment around it to some extent, and people are no exception.

Early people hunted animals.

They extracted metals from rocks in the ground.

After the invention of farming they cleared land for their crops.

By the time of the Ancient Greeks and Romans, some people were beginning to realise that many changes made by humans to the environment were not for the best.

Greek writers remarked on the speed at which the forests were being cut down to make way for grazing land.

A CONSEQUENCE OF CUTTING THE TREES DOWN IS THAT THE TOPSOIL IS WASHED AWAY IN THE RAINS...THIS IS NOT GOOD —

Greek boffin

← Plato

In Ancient Rome the pollution from smoke and dust was so bad that the sun was obscured for much of the time.

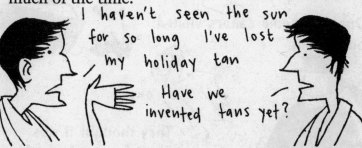

I haven't seen the sun for so long I've lost my holiday tan

Have we invented tans yet?

Neverthless, most people saw the natural world as one vast **resource**, waiting to be exploited by humans.

A resource is a source or supply of something which can be used to fulfill a need

13

Centuries of viewing nature as a vast resource to be exploited to the full had some unfortunate results ...

THE LIFE AND DEATH OF THE DODO

Hello! My name is Dodo. I once lived on the island of Mauritius in the Indian Ocean.

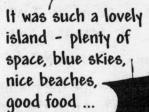

It was such a lovely island – plenty of space, blue skies, nice beaches, good food ...

One day, some sailors visited our island.

They thought it was great fun to chase the dodos. We'd never been chased before! And we couldn't fly!

The sailors killed so many dodos that soon I was the last one left. We became **extinct*** in 1681.

*This is when a whole species of animal or plant dies out.

14

THE LAST PASSENGER PIGEON

Hello, my name is Martha. I was the very last passenger pigeon, but I died in 1914. I lived in Cincinnati Zoo in the US of A, but my brothers and sisters were wild pigeons.

My grandfather used to tell me about old times when there were so many passenger pigeons that the sky was black with our flocks. But all that changed when men started shooting at us. They hunted us for food and for fun.

In about 50 years the hunters shot every single passenger pigeon. The last wild pigeon was popped off by a boy in 1900.

In the past some people did speak out about environmental matters.

St Francis of Assisi (1182-1226) thought that animals, plants and insects had been put on Earth to praise God, and for God's purposes, not simply as a resource for humans.

but it — costs me a fortune in bird seed

Count Georges Louis Leclerc Buffon (1707-88) was one of the first Western scientists to comment on human impact on the environment. He noted the differences between landscapes that had long been inhabited by people, and those as yet untouched.

But it wasn't until the 1960s that more people began to become aware of the impact of human activity on the environment. In 1962, Rachel Carson (1907-1964), an American marine biologist, published a book called *Silent Spring*. She wrote about the harmful effects of pesticides (chemicals used to kill insects that attack crops) on the birds and animals who come into contact with them.

The title of the book describes a spring in which no birds sing because they have all died from the effects of pesticide-poisoning.

Many people disagreed with Rachel Carson's book. But many others listened to her warnings and campaigned against the use of pesticides. The environmental, or 'green', movement was born.

Today, millions of people all around the world are members of environmental organisations, or campaign about environmental issues. Most people know a little about the rainforests, or pollution, or endangered animals, because these are the stories they most often read about. But, in fact, most environmental problems have many different causes and no simple solutions. This book will explain some of the key isues, so YOU can make up your own mind about what can be done.

WHAT IS THE ENVIRONMENT?

Look around you. The environment is:

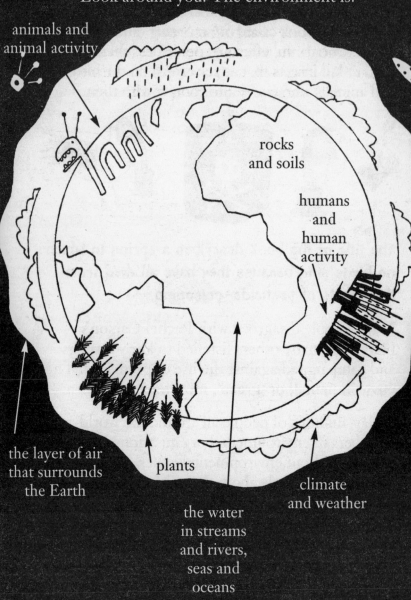

animals and
animal activity

rocks
and soils

humans
and
human
activity

the layer of air
that surrounds
the Earth

plants

climate
and weather

the water
in streams
and rivers,
seas and
oceans

Everything in the environment is connected. The importance of environmental connections was pointed out over 100 years ago by the Scottish scientist, Mary Somerville (1780-1872).
She realised that changing one part of the environment can have unexpected results on other parts: "A farmer sees the rook pecking a little of his grain, or digging at the roots of the springing corn, and poisons all his neighbourhood. A few years after, he is surprised to find his crop destroyed by grubs."

got 'em

The farmer kills the rooks because he thinks they are attacking his crops.

hello

But without any birds to eat the grubs, the grubs flourish and destroy the crops.

SLAP

The farmer did not understand the connection between the rooks and the grubs, so by killing the rooks he disrupted the natural balance between the two.

what have I done?

Some of the most important connections between different parts of the environment are known as **cycles**.

The water cycle

Water is constantly on the move. When water in the oceans, rivers and lakes is heated up it evaporates and turns into vapour. When water droplets in clouds are cooled they fall as rain. This natural cycle goes round and round, continuously recycling water between the oceans, land and air. Water is essential for both plants and animals to survive.

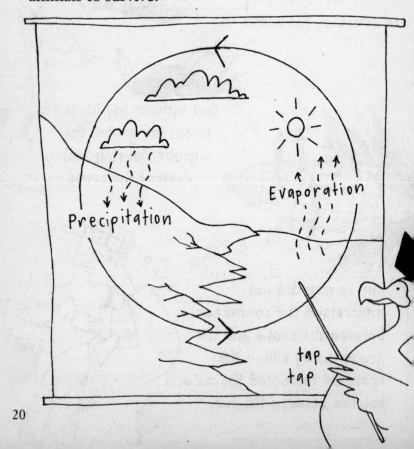

The carbon cycle

Carbon is a chemical element found in different forms in all living things. The biggest carbon stores are contained in rocks and in the oceans. Just as in the water cycle, carbon goes round and round, continuously recycling from one form to another.

Carbon dioxide gas in the air

BURP

Plants and animals contain carbon

Decay of dead plants and animals releases carbon into the ground

Carbon is contained in **fossil fuels**

Plants take carbon from the air to make food in a process called **photosynthesis**

Living things release carbon into the air as part of the process of respiration (breathing)

What is a fossil fuel?

Fossil fuels are coal, oil and natural gas. These are formed over millions of years from the remains of dead plants and animals. See pages 47-49 for more info.

and what exactly is photosynthesis my little plant chum?

I use energy from the sun, carbon dioxide from the air and water from the ground to make carbohydrates (food) and oxygen. I store the carbohydrates to help me grow and I release the oxygen into the air. This is the process called photosynthesis.

21

The environment is often divided up according to **climate**. Some regions of the world have hot, dry climates. Other places have warm, wet climates. Places such as the Arctic and Antarctic have very cold climates. The kind of climate influences the plants and animals that live in the region.

We like it hot!

SLURP

We like it cold!

Scientists study the relationships between living things and their particular environment.
This science is called **ecology**. The complex web of connections linking all the animals and plants in a particular environment is called an **ecosystem**.

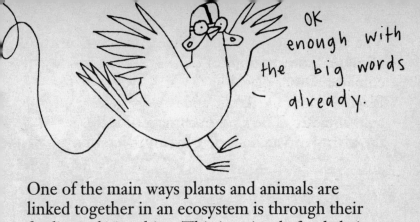

OK enough with the big words already.

One of the main ways plants and animals are linked together in an ecosystem is through their feeding relationships. This is a simple food chain in a forest ecosystem:

Insect grubs eat plants

Small birds and animals eat the grubs

yoo hoo

Hoots

Larger birds, such as owls, eat small birds and animals

In fact, things get more complicated than this. An ecosystem contains many different food chains which all connect to make a vast **food web**.

23

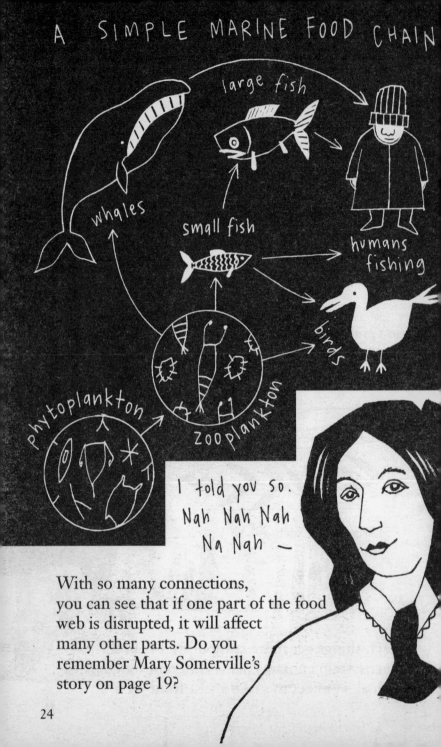

A SIMPLE MARINE FOOD CHAIN

large fish

whales

small fish

humans fishing

phytoplankton

zooplankton

birds

I told you so. Nah Nah Nah Na Nah —

With so many connections, you can see that if one part of the food web is disrupted, it will affect many other parts. Do you remember Mary Somerville's story on page 19?

The connections (cycles, chains, webs) between different parts of the environment form a balance in the natural world. Often human activities disrupt this natural balance. Sometimes, environmental damage by humans is caused by ignorance because we just haven't understood quite how complicated and delicate the balance of the natural world is.

Oh no, not again

DDT

Also, modern ways of life cause huge amounts of waste and pollution.

ackle =
Soon
we shall
rule
the world

GLOBAL
NASTY
COMPANY
HAVE A NICE DAY

25

The huge differences in the way people live across the globe also affects the environment. Most damaging is the general relationship between the **developing** countries of the 'Third World' and the **developed** countries of the 'First World'.

The First/developed countries of the world can also be called the rich countries. These are countries with successful, developed industries and generally high standards of living.

Did you know that, on average, children in the USA are given more pocket money in a year than some workers in the poorest countries earn in a year?

The Third/developing countries are the poorer countries of the world. Many have little industry, and the standard of living is generally low.

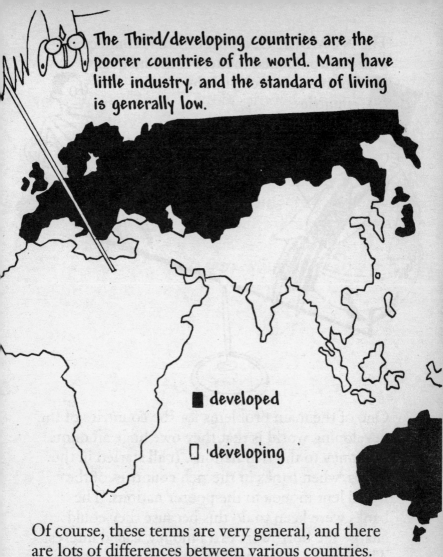

■ developed

☐ developing

Of course, these terms are very general, and there are lots of differences between various countries. For instance, some developing countries are too poor to spend any money on developing their industry, others are able to invest in industry and raise their standards of living. And even in the poorest countries some people are well-off, just as in the richest countries there are often people living in extreme poverty.

27

The NUMBER ONE BIG ISSUE connected with environmental matters is the inequality between the rich and the poorer countries.

One of the main problems for the countries of the developing world is that they owe huge amounts of money to the rich nations. It all started in the 1970s, when banks in the rich countries of the world lent money to the poorer nations. The banks were keen to do this because they could charge the borrowers extra money, called interest. The banks were certain that they would get their original money back, plus all the interest as well.

But as the debts got bigger and bigger, so did the amount of interest. In the 1980s it became clear that many poor countries simply couldn't pay off all their debts. Some countries could not even afford the interest payments on their debts.

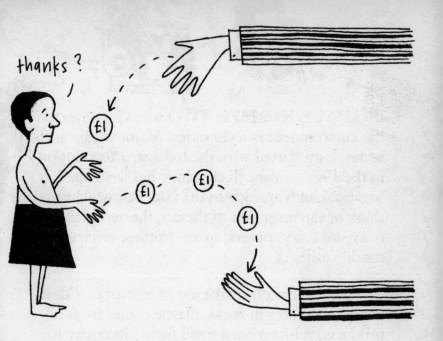

thanks?

£1

£1 £1

£1

Most developing countries continue to pay millions of pounds to the banks to try to repay their debts. Meanwhile, these countries cannot afford proper health care or education for their people. To try to help them set up these basic services the governments of many rich countries give some money as aid to the developing countries . But is this really the answer? The figures speak for themselves: for every £1 given in aid to the developing countries in 1993 the rich nations took back £3 in debt repayments.

This is all important for the environment because it is sometimes tempting to blame governments and people in the poor countries for environmental destruction. But as we shall see, these people often have little choice.

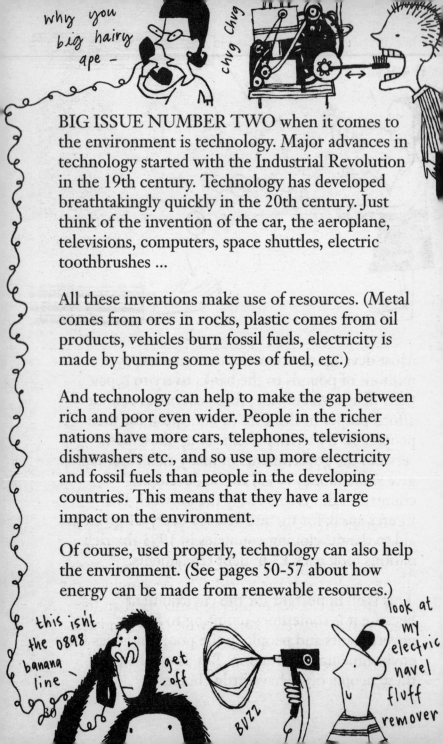

why you big hairy ape —

chug chug

BIG ISSUE NUMBER TWO when it comes to the environment is technology. Major advances in technology started with the Industrial Revolution in the 19th century. Technology has developed breathtakingly quickly in the 20th century. Just think of the invention of the car, the aeroplane, televisions, computers, space shuttles, electric toothbrushes ...

All these inventions make use of resources. (Metal comes from ores in rocks, plastic comes from oil products, vehicles burn fossil fuels, electricity is made by burning some types of fuel, etc.)

And technology can help to make the gap between rich and poor even wider. People in the richer nations have more cars, telephones, televisions, dishwashers etc., and so use up more electricity and fossil fuels than people in the developing countries. This means that they have a large impact on the environment.

Of course, used properly, technology can also help the environment. (See pages 50-57 about how energy can be made from renewable resources.)

this isn't the 0898 banana line

get off

BUZZ

look at my electric navel fluff remover

BIG ISSUE NUMBER THREE is population.

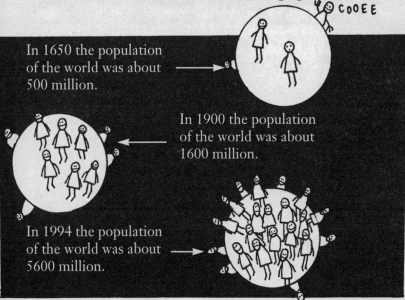

In 1650 the population of the world was about 500 million.

In 1900 the population of the world was about 1600 million.

In 1994 the population of the world was about 5600 million.

In the 250 years between 1650 and 1900 the number of people in the world trebled. In the 94 years between 1900 and 1994 the number of people in the world more than trebled again. The speed at which the number of people in the world increases is called the **population growth rate**.

There are many reasons for the increase in the population growth rate. Technology has played a part in improving food production and medicine. But population growth is not evenly spread across all the countries of the world. The developing countries have faster population growth than the developed countries. (Turn to page 90 to find out why.) More people use more resources and produce more waste. This has an impact on the environment.

It seems that humans truly are the environmental baddies! But the natural world sometimes comes up with spectacular events that make human actions look positively puny!

Air pollution is a major problem in many parts of the world (see pages 34-45). But the prize for some of the most sensational air pollution goes to the world's volcanoes.

March - April 1982: El Chichón, Mexico
Three huge explosions. Avalanches of molten rock pour down the mountainside, killing more than 1,000 people. Vast clouds of gas and ash shoot over 25 kilometres into the sky. Three weeks later the cloud of ash has blown right around the Earth. Many scientists believe that this ash cloud disrupted world climate patterns, causing drought in Australia and heavy rain in California, USA.

Humans manufacture some powerful poisons, but nature can come up with equally lethal substances.

August 21, 1986: Lake Nyos, Cameroon, West Africa
A poisonous cloud suffocates over 1700 people. The cloud came from Lake Nyos, a small lake in a volcanic crater. Gases from the volcano had become trapped in the lake. On the night of August 21, a small explosion released these gases into the air. The lethal cloud rolled silently down the valley towards the town of Lower Nyos, killing both humans and animals.

Natural hazard quiz
There are many other natural hazards that can cause huge amounts of environmental destruction and chaos. Can you fill in the missing letters to complete this list of natural hazards?

E * * * * q * * * *
A * a * a * * * *
L * * h t * * n *
* o * * a d *

* u * s l * * *
* * o o *
H * r r * * * * *
T s * * * * i

Answers
Earthquake, mudslide, avalanche, flood, lightning, hurricane, tornado, tsunami (huge tidal wave)

33

BEHIND THE HEADLINES

To find out what's really happening in the environment, we need to go behind the headlines ...

What's the missing link between:
1. This

and this?

2. Or this

and this

3. Or this

and this?

Read on to find out ...

ACID RAIN

The term 'acid rain' was first used in the 1850s by a chemist called R.A. Smith. He tested the rain in and around Manchester and found that it contained an unusually high amount of sulphuric acid. He suspected this might have something to do with the coal-burning factories nearby ...

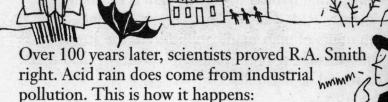

DONG DONG

Over 100 years later, scientists proved R.A. Smith right. Acid rain does come from industrial pollution. This is how it happens:

hmmm

Pollution from many factories, power stations and car exhausts contains sulphur and nitrogen.

The sulphur and nitrogen react with water, sunlight and oxygen in the atmosphere to form acid rain.

Acid rain often falls many hundreds of kilometres away from the original source of the pollution.

Acid rain pollutes rivers and lakes, kills wildlife, and can damage buildings.

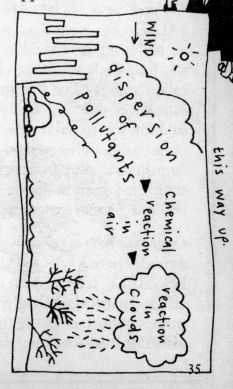

WIND

dispersion of pollutants

chemical reaction in air

reaction in clouds

this way up.

35

True or false?
Mr. Factbuster is here
to tell you
the truth about
acid rain ...

Rain is naturally acid.
TRUE. There are many
natural sources of sulphur
(volcanic eruptions, the oceans) and nitrogen
(lightning, natural decay), so rain is normally
slightly acid. But human activities add huge
amounts of man-made pollution to the atmosphere, making rain in many places more acid than
it would be naturally.

The problem can be solved by building higher chimneys.
FALSE – but it has been tried! In the early 1950s
air pollution was so bad in London that the city
was frequently smothered by thick pollution-fogs,
called 'smogs'. The British government
introduced new laws to clean up the air. One
solution was to build taller chimneys so that
industrial pollution would go high into the
atmosphere, away from the local area. But this has
simply led to air pollution – and acid rain –
becoming a more widespread problem.

*Coniferous trees suffer more from acid rain than
deciduous trees.*
POSSIBLY. It seems that coniferous forests are
affected particularly badly by acid rain. The acid
washes important nutrients (plant food) out of the
soil. The trees lose their needles and slowly die.

Some scientists once thought that acid rain was a good thing.
TRUE. Both sulphur and nitrogen are essential minerals for plant growth. About 20 years ago, some scientists put forward the theory that the added minerals in acid rain would help crops to grow. But it seems that acid rain is more likely to cause harm than do good.

The effects of acid rain are worse in some areas than in others.
TRUE. Europe and North America are the regions worse affected by acid rain. This is because of the large amounts of industry in these areas. Locally, the effects of acid rain depend upon the type of plants, soil and rocks that the rain falls on. Some rocks and soils can absorb the effects of acid rain much better than others.

Acid rain eats buildings!
TRUE. The acid eats into the stone. Scientists say that more damage has been done to the stone of the ancient monuments of Athens, Greece, in the last 30 years than in the whole of the previous 2000 years of their existence.

Liming is the answer ...
TRUE and FALSE. In Scandinavia, lime is sprayed on lakes that have been badly affected by acid rain. The lime helps to neutralise the acid in the lake water. But this is no long-term solution. Many countries are now taking measures to try to reduce the amount of air pollution produced by industry and by cars.

THE OZONE LAYER

Date: October 1982
Place: Halley Bay, Antarctica

Dr Joe Farman and his team check the readings on their scientific instruments. They are measuring the amount of ozone in the sky above them.

I can't believe it! There must be something wrong. Maybe the reading is wrong...

one year later... I replaced the meter but the reading's still low...

another year later... There is definitely something going on up there...

In 1985, Dr Joe Farman reported that he had found a huge hole in the layer of **ozone** that surrounds the Earth. The hole lay over Antarctica. The report caused a sensation.
What had caused the hole? And what effect would it have?

what is ozone?

Ozone is a gas. Each molecule* of ozone is three oxygen atoms* stuck together. Most ozone gas lies high up in the Earth's atmosphere, in a wide band between about ten and 50 kilometres above your head. This is often called the 'ozone layer'.

The ozone layer absorbs some of the rays from the sun, stopping them from reaching the Earth. These rays are called ultraviolet (UV) light. Humans need some UV to keep healthy, and it is UV light that gives pale skins a tan. But there are fears that too much UV can be harmful to human skin, in some cases causing skin cancer.

what does it do?

In fact, scientists have found two holes: one over the Antarctic and a smaller one over the Arctic. They have linked the appearance of the holes with various man-made chemicals. The most well-known of these are the chlorofluorocarbons, or **CFCs**.

what caused the hole in the ozone layer?

* An atom is the smallest part of a chemical element. A molecule is a group of atoms joined together. All matter is made up of atoms and molecules.

CFCs are very useful chemicals.

Hello! I'm a CFC molecule made up of chlorine, fluoride and carbon atoms.
* I don't burn
* I don't react with other gases
* I'm cheap to produce
* I am used for many different things: in fridges, in air-conditioning units, in aerosols, to blow up foams for the insides of furniture, to make fast-food containers.

* I have no smell
* I'm not poisonous
* I'm easy to store

At ground level CFCs don't break up or react with other gases. But the problems start when CFC molecules are released into the air and gradually drift upwards into the Earth's atmosphere. It takes eight to ten years for a CFC molecule to reach the ozone layer. Then intense UV light from the sun does break up the CFC molecule and makes it react with the ozone. Every CFC molecule destroys thousands of ozone molecules in the ozone layer.

ACTION! ACTION!
September 1987: 36 nations sign an agreement called the Montreal Protocol agreeing to cut the use of CFCs.
June 1990: Montreal Protocol revised. New agreement to stop CFC production by 2000. More nations sign.

When the story about the ozone hole hit the headlines it seemed simple – 'baddy' chemicals (CFCs) destroying the natural protective ozone layer around the Earth. Under pressure from governments and popular opinion, chemical companies agreed to cut the use of CFCs and to develop different, less harmful, chemicals to replace them. But is the story so simple?

Ozone and CFCs

Factbusters

CFCs are the only 'ozone-eaters'.
FALSE. Other man-made chemicals such as HCFCs (hydrochlorofluorocarbons) and halons (used in fire extinguishers) also destroy ozone. But some of the main ozone-eaters come from natural sources such as rotting wood, fires and volcanic eruptions.

The ozone layer is the same thickness all around the Earth.
FALSE. The thickness of the ozone layer is constantly changing, depending upon the time of day and the season.

The ozone layer protects life on Earth from the harmful effects of sunlight.
TRUE. The ozone layer absorbs most of the (UV) part of sunlight that reaches the Earth. What happens as the ozone layer becomes thinner? The answer is that no one knows for certain. If more UV light reaches Earth more people could get skin cancer, plant growth could be affected, and some scientists think that life in the world's oceans might be damaged too.

The holes in the ozone will quickly repair themselves.
FALSE. CFCs are so long-lasting that even if all CFC production stopped today, it is likely to take more than 100 years for the ozone layer to repair itself. However, cutting down the number of CFCs will help to slow down the damage to the ozone layer.

GLOBAL WARMING

Not only are CFCs ozone-eaters, they are also members of the **greenhouse gases** club.

Welcome to the greenhouse! The average temperature of the Earth is controlled naturally by a whole collection of natural greenhouse gases. They are called greenhouse gases because:

1. They are in the Earth's atmosphere.
2. They allow sunlight (light and heat energy) through.
3. Light and heat energy reflect off the Earth's surface.
4. The greenhouse gases trap the heat energy, just like the glass in a greenhouse traps heat inside but allows light to pass through.

good
for
tomat
thou

Without the natural control of the greenhouse gases the Earth would be 33°C cooler, and life on Earth would be quite different! Gases in the greenhouse club include:

Captain Carbon Dioxide

Nitrous Oxide Man

Miss Methane

Water Vapour Woman

In the last 100 years human activities have added huge amounts of greenhouse gases to the Earth's atmosphere. New gases such as CFCs have also been added.

The most important of the greenhouse gases is carbon dioxide. Humans add carbon dioxide to the Earth's atmosphere by burning fossil fuels (coal, oil, gas) for transport, for heat, or in power stations to make electricity; also by burning down forests; and other processes such as cement manufacture.

There is no doubt that the amount of carbon dioxide in the Earth's atmosphere has increased dramatically. What scientists cannot agree on is the effect this will have.

Predicting the future

More carbon dioxide in the atmosphere means that more heat is being trapped around the Earth. This is backed up by measurements which show that the temperature of the air around Earth has risen by 0.5°C in the last 100 years. This effect has been called **global warming**.

Global warming could touch the lives of everyone on planet Earth.

Ice would melt and cause sea levels to rise. Low-lying coastlines and islands could be flooded.(For instance, Bangladesh, Pacific Islands, the Maldives.)

do you have an ice lolly?

Large numbers of icebergs could break off ice sheets causing danger to ships.

hot enough for ya?

Climates could change, in some places becoming hotter, in some places wetter. This will affect the kinds of crops that can be grown, and could threaten food supplies.

No one can predict exactly what effects global warming will have in the future. But it is obvious that human action is having some influence on the world's climate. Some scientists think that Earth will recover naturally. Others predict disastrous consequences. It would be safer to cut down NOW on the greenhouse gases we pump into the atmosphere, but this isn't as simple as it sounds (as we'll go on to find out) ...

glug

TITANIC

miow

pocket alarm

HOOT

pet bed heater

lava lamp

geiger counter

hammond organ

Dull emitter triode

HOW MANY DIFFERENT ENERGY CONSUMING DEVICES HAVE YOU USED TODAY?

Energy is the power that makes cells develop, plants grow and machines move. It comes from burning fuel. For instance, the sun is a ball of burning gases which gives off huge amounts of heat and light energy. We also burn energy in the cells inside our bodies.

The modern world is driven by energy-consuming machines. Some machines run on energy from burning fuels (such as cars, which burn petrol or diesel). Other machines, such as computers, use electricity - which is itself made by burning some kind of fuel.

Much of the energy we use comes from the sun. Energy from the sun is essential to life on Earth. Plants use the energy in sunlight to make food and grow (in a process called photosynthesis - see page 21). Animals eat the plants. Other animals eat the animals that ate the plants. Each time, the energy is passed on.

Fossil fuels are the remains of plants and animals that died millions of years ago. When we burn fossil fuels we are releasing sun-energy that is millions of years old!

pardon me

CHECKLIST OF FOSSIL FUELS:

- coal
- oil
- natural gas

Fossil fuels are **non-renewable**. This means that the supplies of coal, oil and gas will eventually run out.

what do you mean none left?

It's gone

When fossil fuels are burned they release the greenhouse gas carbon dioxide (see page 43). They also release sulphur and nitrogen, causing acid rain (see page 35). We rely on fossil fuels to drive our cars and make our electricity. It makes sense to use fossil fuels - in fact, all fuels - as **efficiently** as possible so that we conserve supplies, and we don't pollute the atmosphere any more than we need to. But, often, this is not what happens ...

EFFICIENCY means achieving something by using up as little of a resource as possible, while producing as little waste as possible. In other words, less is more!

Sad Tales of Waste

I, the local efficiency sleuth, have uncovered some criminal tales of waste. I am on a mission to solve the mystery of the lost energy. My first task is to discover how efficiently we turn fossil fuels into electricity. I find that at least 60% of the energy contained in this coal is wasted in the process of turning it into electricity.

COAL

My next case is a particularly horrifying one! Did you know that the amount of energy used to heat this house could be reduced by at least 50% if the windows, doors and loft were insulated to stop heat escaping?

Im too Hot Now

Tsk Tsk

I thought that the purpose of a light bulb was to make light! But I find that this bulb uses up almost as much energy making heat as it does light. What a waste!

Renewable energy is energy which comes from sources that cannot be used up.

RENEWABLE ENERGY CHECKLIST:

- wind power
- hydropower
- wave power
- tide power
- solar energy
- biomass
- geothermal energy

Many people would like to see more of the world's energy being made from renewable sources. Renewable energy has many advantages, so why isn't more effort made to make use of these sources?

Windpower

Wind energy has been used for centuries to power sailing boats and windmills. Modern windmills, called turbines, are used to generate electricity.

FOR: In certain places, wind energy is fairly constant. Generating electricity from windpower produces no pollution.

AGAINST: Large commercial windfarms take up a lot of space, and the turbines need to be in windy places such as the tops of hills or on seashores, so they can't be hidden away. Many people object to the idea of a landscape covered in windmills!

Hydropower

Hydropower is the energy from fast-running or falling water. The movement of the water turns turbines which generate electricity. Electricity made from water power is called hydroelectricity.

FOR: Many countries already have large hydroelectric schemes. Water power is constant, and it produces no pollution.

AGAINST: Hydroelectric projects often involve building huge dams, and flooding large areas of land. This can have a major effect both on the environment and the people in the area.

51

Wave and tide power

Wave power uses the movement of waves on the sea to generate electricity. Tide power uses the movement of water caused by the tides to generate electricity.

FOR: Energy from the movement of the oceans is constant and it produces no pollution.

AGAINST: In order to harness the energy of tides and waves it is necessary to build barrages. As the water passes through these barrages it turns turbines which generate electricity. The barrages alter the way the water flows in and out of estuaries, or around shorelines. This has an effect on the coastal environment and can damage marine life.

Solar power

Heat energy from the sun can be used directly in various ways to heat buildings. This is called solar energy.

FOR: Energy from the sun can be used to heat water in solar panels to supply heating systems. Solar power can also be used to generate electricity. Even in places where the sky is often quite cloudy (like the UK!), there is still enough solar energy getting through to make a difference. More research needs to be done, but solar power is one of the main ways forward for the future.

AGAINST: In very cloudy places it can't be used as the only system for making energy.

Biomass is the best.

it's certainly the smelliest.

Biomass

Biomass is another word for plant material. Wood, animal dung and gases from rotting rubbish can all be burnt to produce heat or electricity.

FOR: Some countries make good use of biomass gases to generate electricity. A fuel made from sugar cane can be used as an alternative to petrol for powering cars. Fuelwood and dung are major sources of heat energy in many developing countries. Biomass fuels make good use of waste products, and are cleaner than burning fossil fuels.

AGAINST: In many developing countries the use of wood for fuel has led to **deforestation** (see page 59).

Best toaster there is —

HOT SPOT ↓

Geothermal power

Geothermal energy is heat energy from rocks beneath the surface of the Earth.

FOR: In countries such as Iceland, heat energy from inside the Earth is easily tapped. Hot water is brought from a few kilometres beneath the surface and used for large-scale heating systems.

AGAINST: This form of energy produces some air pollution, as gases from inside the Earth are brought to the surface and released into the atmosphere. It's cleaner than burning fossil fuels, though.

Yet another form of energy is **nuclear power**, which is mainly used to generate electricity. This form of energy comes from atoms of a metal called uranium. (In theory, supplies of uranium will, one day, run out, so nuclear power is non-renewable.) A tiny particle called a neutron is fired at the uranium atom, which then splits, releasing its energy. This is called **nuclear fission**.

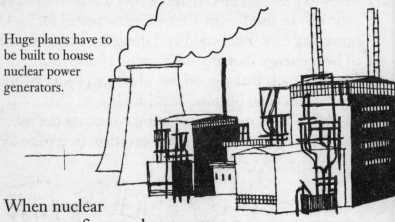

Huge plants have to be built to house nuclear power generators.

When nuclear power was first used to generate electricity in the 1950s, people thought that it was safe and clean. Now they are not so sure. Every time a uranium atom splits it also gives off radioactive radiation. High doses of radioactive radiation can kill humans and other animals. Low doses can cause leukaemia and other kinds of cancer. Virtually everything that touches a nuclear reactor becomes radioactive, and therefore dangerous. Despite all precautions, radioactive materials do sometimes leak out into the environment. There have been many small radioactive leaks, and some more major ones.

eek

another type of large plant →

Chernobyl

A turning-point in the nuclear story came in 1986
when there was a serious accident at a nuclear power
station at Chernobyl, in the Ukraine (then part of
the USSR). There had been nuclear accidents
before, but not on the scale of Chernobyl ...

On 26 April 1986, engineers in reactor
no.4 at the Chernobyl power station
were testing their emergency systems.
Something went wrong and the reactor
blew up. Two engineers died in the
explosion.

For ten days helicopters
dumped lead and sand on the
burning reactor to try to put
out the fire in the reactor.

The explosion sent out a cloud of
radioactivity which reached many
parts of the USSR and Europe,
including the UK. The radioactivity
was eventually detected as far away
as Washington, USA and Tokyo,
Japan.

An area 64 kilometres wide
around Chernobyl was evacuated.
Contaminated livestock were
killed, crops destroyed, topsoil
removed and trees cut down.
Radiation affected animals and
plants further afield, too ...

Ten years later the full effects of the accident are
still not known. Over 200,000 people were moved
from their homes and have had to start new lives
in strange towns. No one knows how many people
have died from diseases caused by radiation, or
from the stress caused by the accident and its
aftermath.

So is nuclear power safe?

Because of the risks, in most countries the nuclear industry is very strictly controlled. But there is always the danger of accidents. There have been reports of an increase in the number of people with cancer living near nuclear power stations, but scientists have not established a definite link between the two.

And is it clean?

The process of making electricity from nuclear power may not give off smoke and fumes into the atmosphere like fossil fuels do. But it does produce radioactive waste. Different countries have different ways to dispose of this, depending on how contaminated the waste is: some waste is discharged into the sea, some is buried underground, some is stored on the surface.

Despite the best efforts of the nuclear industry, many people are deeply suspicious of nuclear power. No matter how tightly controlled nuclear reactors are, there will always be some danger of accident. The question of what to do with outdated nuclear power plants and radioactive waste has not been satisfactorily answered for many people. Many countries have stopped investing in new nuclear power stations. However millions of pounds are still spent on the nuclear industry. Maybe this money would be better spent on developing renewable alternatives instead?

So who uses what?

ENERGY FACTS

* The developed countries rely largely on fossil fuels to supply their huge energy needs. They are the energy-guzzlers of the world. They contain less than 25% of the world's population, yet they use more than 70% of the world's fossil fuels.

* It's been estimated that the average person in the UK uses up ten times more energy than the average person in India.

* While people in the developed world are busy consuming fossil fuels, people in the poorer countries of the developing world rely on biomass fuels such as wood, charcoal and dung for their energy needs.

It is up to the people of the developed world to:
• use less energy
• use energy more efficiently
• find and use ways to produce energy that are less harmful to the environment than fossil fuels
• spend money on setting up renewable sources of energy.

It won't be easy! Take up the challenge!

To take you on a journey through
this next section, I would like to
introduce a distant cousin
of mine - the macaw.

**Welcome to my home, the
beautiful rainforest.**

What is a rainforest? It's easy really.
It's a forest that has lots of rain -
more than four metres every year.
That's more than six times the amount
you get in the UK! The rainforests of the
world grow in the hot, wet climate in the tropics
(which is why they are often called tropical
rainforests). There are three main areas:

in West and
Central Africa

in Central and
South America

in South-east Asia

The largest rainforest in the world is the Amazon
in South America. It's larger than all the other
rainforests put together.

Rainforests hit the headlines regularly because they are disappearing! Every year, people cut down or burn large areas of rainforest. This process is called **deforestation**. But why is this so important?

... because of the vast number of animals and plants rainforests contain - over half of all the known species (types) of animals and plants in the whole world (including the smelliest plant). And this is only counting the species you humans know about. There are unknown thousands of rainforest species yet to be identified ...

... because of the links between rainforests and the Earth's climate. Scientists think that cutting down rainforest trees could disrupt the water cycle (see page 20) and make droughts more likely. Burning rainforests also releases the greenhouse gas (see page 42), carbon dioxide, into the air (but not as much as comes from burning fossil fuels).

... because of the hundreds of products humans get from rainforests including: the raw products for medicines; food plants such as coffee, tea, pineapples, avocados, bananas and brazil nuts; and raw materials such as rubber, palm oil and timber.

... because rainforests are home to millions of people who have lived there for centuries.

here the NS r rots

On a personal note, the rainforest is my home and I'm very happy there

SEED

SAVE OUR TREES!

Many thousands of years ago, much of Europe and North America was covered in dense forest. Much of this was cut or burned down to make way for farming land, so there is very little left today. Who knows how many animal and plant species were wiped out? Now these developed countries want the developing countries (where many of the rainforest regions are found) to stop destroying their forests. But like most issues connected to the environment, the reasons for the destruction of the rainforest are not simple. It's easy to see the people who cut down or burn rainforests simply as 'baddies'. But let's look behind the headline stories so you can decide for yourself.

1. Farmers. Local forest peoples have farmed in the rainforests for thousands of years. They have developed a method of farming that suits their rainforest surroundings. They clear a small patch of land to grow crops such as cassava, rice and sago. When the land is exhausted they clear another small plot in a different part of the forest. The rainforest gradually grows back across the first plot and its fertility is largely restored. This is called **shifting cultivation**.

O BOY
O BOY

2. Timber loggers. The rainforests are sources of precious hardwood such as rosewood and mahogany. The loggers build roads into remote areas of rainforest. They then remove the valuable trees. Unfortunately, the heavy machinery used to take out these trees leaves a trail of destruction behind. The wood is sold abroad to the rich developed nations. Governments of the developing countries often encourage logging because it is a source of much-needed income.

four stomachs means four puddings you know.

3. Ranchers. The rainforest is cut or burned down to make space for cattle ranches. This has happened particularly in Central and South America. In some cases, the meat is sold to the richer, developed countries to provide cheap meat for burgers and other food products. Unfortunately the poor soil quickly loses its fertility, and many ranches have to be abandoned after a few years.

4. Settlers. As the loggers and ranchers move in, clearing forest and making new roads, others follow. For many years, governments have seen the rainforests as 'a land without people, for a people without land'. They have encouraged poor people to settle in rainforest regions, promising a better life. These people are forced to cut down more rainforest to grow their crops, and to try to eke out a living.

True or false? Some of the things you may not know about **rainforest deforestation** ...

The rainforest soil is ideal for growing crops.

FALSE: Surprisingly, rainforest soils are very poor and infertile. All the nutrients needed to make plants grow are in the plants themselves. This means that when the rainforest is cleared to grow crops, the soil is quickly exhausted. The traditional forest peoples have long understood this, which is why they practice shifting cultivation (see page 60).

Deforestation can lead to erosion.

TRUE: The leaves of rainforest trees protect the thin soil below from the heavy tropical rains that fall almost every day. When this protective layer is removed, the thin layer of soil is quickly washed away. This process is called **erosion**.

It doesn't matter if we destroy a few rainforest species every now and then does it?

FALSE: It matters for many reasons, not least that we don't know how useful an unknown rainforest plant may one day be to humans! Many rainforest plants already form the basis for medicines, and many thousands more are being tested for possible use. We now grow useful food plants, such as tea, coffee and bananas, on plantations, but did you know that they were originally found in rainforests?

The traditional peoples of the forest are in as much danger as the rainforest plants and animals.
TRUE: The main threats are from ranchers, miners, loggers and new settlers who (often backed by the government) move in to the rain-forest peoples' lands, destroying their traditional way of life. In some places, there are plans for large hydroelectric schemes (see page 51), which would flood huge areas of rainforest, destroying vast expanses of homeland. The new workers and settlers bring with them diseases, such as influenza and measles, unknown to the local people, which can kill them.

At this rate, the Amazon rainforest will have completely disappeared by the year 2010 ...
FALSE: It is very difficult to get accurate figures about deforestation. Scientists use satellite pictures to try to calculate data about the world's forests. It is unlikely that the Amazon rainforest is being cut down at such a rate. However, the destruction continues in the Amazon, and in other areas of rainforest around the world.

Rainforest solutions

The *simple* answer to the world's rainforest problems would be to make all the rainforests protected areas and to keep all the people out.

KEEP OUT
trespassers
will be
prosecuted

But too many people rely on the rainforest for their living for this approach to work. Anyway, the Amazon rainforest is 6 million sq km - imagine trying to keep people out of an area of land this size! So, rainforest solutions must take into account the needs of people and of the environment.

One of the main ways forward is **sustainable management**. This means making use of forest resources without causing long-term damage. Traditional forest peoples have practiced sustainable methods of farming for centuries (shifting cultivation). Today, it is possible to make a good living from the rainforests by harvesting nuts, fruits and rubber for sale locally or abroad.

Much of the damage to the rainforest is caused because of short-term profit. Most timber companies are more interested in making money fast than in preserving the rainforest environment. But in 1986, timber companies from all over the world became members of ITTO (the International Tropical Timber Organization). One of the aims of this organisation is to encourage better management of the world's rainforest resources.

Lastly, the developed countries of the world must be prepared to pay their share for saving the rain-forests. Many developing countries owe vast amounts of money to developed countries. Governments of these developing countries can't afford *not* to make use of their rainforest resources because they need money to pay off these debts. Some countries have agreed to swap their debts for nature. This means that in return for a reduction in the amount of a debt, a rainforest country agrees to conserve an area of forest.

Sounds great doesn't it? But it only works if the local people are involved right from the start -
after all, the forest is their home, and they have to survive too ...

MUDDYING THE WATERS

For this next section we're going underwater. I never learned to swim, so I'm handing you over to an expert - the dolphin.

This is my watery world: the seas and oceans. Living in the sea is rather different from living on land. Let me tell you some sea and ocean facts ...

The seas and oceans cover 71% of the Earth's surface.

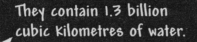

They contain 1.3 billion cubic kilometres of water.

In some places the ocean is more than 11 kilometres deep.

The largest ocean, the Pacific, covers five times the area of the African continent.

Wow! Frend was Right.

Only the top layer of water enjoys sunlight. Below about 100 metres it is constantly dark.

The seas and oceans of the world form a huge ecosystem (see page 22) about which humans know relatively little. This is because it is very difficult for people to explore the ocean depths. However, humans have long regarded the seas and oceans as a useful resource. The seas and oceans are vital sources of food. And just as in the rainforests, scientists are beginning to realise the importance of the huge number of marine life forms for medicine and for industry.

Burp

The average person in Japan eats 66.6 kilograms of fish every year!

Some tiny ocean animals are being used to develop medicines to fight cancer.

Now for a closer look at what people take out of the seas and oceans and how they do it.

Fishing has provided people with a source of food for centuries. Traditional methods of fishing meant that it was only possible to catch a limited number of fish.

But technological developments in modern fishing methods, combined with an increase in demand for fish (because of population growth) means that stocks of fish are disappearing. Fishing is now an industry. Huge commercial fishing boats travel thousands of kilometres away from their home ports, and stay away for weeks and months at a time. As the fish are caught, they are frozen to keep them fresh until the ship returns to port.

You might think that industrial fishing would be very efficient. But many modern fishing methods are very wasteful. For instance, shrimp trawling nets scrape everything off the seabed, not just shrimp. The unwanted fish and shellfish are then thrown back - mostly dead.

Tuna fish are usually caught in a huge circular net called a purse seine. But until recently, because tuna and dolphin often swim together, thousands of dolphins were becoming entangled in the seine nets and dying. Now,

where's all the fish?
it's a complicated — global issue comrade.

thanks to a campaign to save the dolphin, many fishing ships use 'dolphin friendly' nets.

The problem of overfishing affects animals and birds: as fish become scarcer, so deaths from starvation increase. Overfishing affects people too. Local people in many developing countries rely on fish to feed themselves and their families. Many are finding it more and more difficult to catch enough fish, and are being forced to travel far from their local fishing grounds.

SOLUTIONS?
- Quotas – each ship only allowed to catch so many fish
- More efficient fishing methods
- Reduce the fishing fleet
- Shorten seasons when fishing is allowed

These solutions are in force in different places around the world, but all have their drawbacks. No one knows if they will be enough to allow the fish stocks to recover.

Coral reefs are some of the richest environments beneath the waves. They are made up from the skeletons of millions of tiny animals called polyps. Reefs are found only in tropical seas, and they are home to thousands of different species. Because of this, coral reefs have been called the 'rainforests of the oceans'.

Here's how and why people destroy coral reefs.

BLAST-FISHING: Blowing up the reef with dynamite to release fish hidden inside.

POISON: Local people make some much-needed cash by spraying poison around the reef to stun the exotic fish that live there. The fish are caught and exported to be sold to aquarium enthusiasts.

TOURISM: Tourists are often allowed to dive down to reefs. A few tourists every year won't do much harm. But in some places reefs have been badly damaged by thousands of divers bumping into the coral, holding on to it or standing on it. Coral is also removed from the reef to sell as tourist souvenirs.

DEFORESTATION: When trees are cut down on land, the result is often soil erosion (see page 62). The soil washes into rivers, and from there into the sea, covering coral reefs with a layer of sediment and smothering the life of the reef.

The tale of the whale (but what about the plankton?)

Whales have been hunted by coastal peoples for thousands of years. Traditionally, whale blubber was used to provide oil for light and heat, and whale meat was an important source of food. In the 19th and 20th centuries whaling became big business. Large whaling fleets caught thousands of whales every year.

The earliest efforts to control the number of whales being caught began in the 1930s. But it wasn't until the 1980s that whaling was almost completely banned.

Whales are large, beautiful creatures, so it's relatively easy to raise public concern about their disappearance. But what about the tiny life forms in the oceans such as plankton or worms? We are less glamorous, but just as important.*

The whaling ban was due largely to a successful campaign fought by organisations such as Friends of the Earth and Greenpeace which was widely supported by the public. Today, some countries continue to hunt small numbers of whales (Norway and Japan in particular). But 'whale-watching' (trips to watch whales) has become one of the fastest-growing tourist industries, in many places making a live whale worth much more than a dead one ...

*See pages 85-89 for more about disappearing species.

Marine pollution

Of course, this is only what people take OUT of the seas. The second half of the story is what we put IN. Many people seem to view my home as one huge dustbin! Into the seas and oceans go: sewage, industrial waste, waste from farming, rubbish from ships, oil leaks and spills, plastic waste, nuclear waste, air pollution from chimneys and car exhausts ...

OIL SPILL BLACKENS BEACHES - RESCUE OPERATION TO SAVE OILED BIRDS

Oil spill accidents such as the *Torrey Canyon* off the coast of Cornwall, or the *Exxon Valdez* off the coast of Alaska, receive huge amounts of publicity in the newspapers and on television because they are so dramatic. They cause long-term damage to the local environment (for instance, some experts think that it can take up to 25 years for wildlife to recover from an oil spill such as the *Exxon Valdez*), and the effects are easy to see: black beaches, dead and oiled birds, dead seals and other wildlife. But if we look behind the headlines, we soon find that there is another story to be told which is much less dramatic, but more harmful to the ocean environment.

DOG FOUND TO BE GUILTY OF BARKING

Invisible pollution

Did you know that more marine pollution is caused by agriculture than by oil spills? Many farmers put fertilisers on their fields to make the crops grow, and spray their fields with pesticides to kill off insect pests. When it rains, the chemicals in these fertilisers and pesticides are washed away into streams and rivers. These chemicals eventually end up in the sea.

One of the most famous of the pesticides is called DDT. When it gets into the ocean, DDT is taken in by tiny animals such as plankton. It then passes through the marine food chain (see page 24) to large birds such as cormorants and peregrine falcons. The DDT in the birds' bodies makes them lay eggs with very thin shells, so that the eggs break very easily. DDT is now banned in most developed countries, but it is still made and sold to many developing countries, where the controls over pesticides are less strict.

The oceans and seas are so vast that in the past they managed to dilute and absorb much of the waste that humans dumped into them. But the development of industry and modern methods of farming, and the increase in the human population have all meant more pollution heading out seawards.

Bogus

Most of the chemicals that humans put into the sea are found there naturally anyway. So what is the problem, you might ask? It's all a question of balance. Change one part of the ecosystem and everything else changes too (see page 19).

A question of balance

Calcium, magnesium, nitrogen, phosphorus, potassium, sulphur ... all these nutrients are vital for marine life. But if the balance of nutrients is disrupted, this has a knock-on effect.

OXYGEN

Phosphorus and nitrogen are present in pollution from fertilisers, sewage and industrial waste. The natural balance of phosphorus and nitrogen in the water is upset by the added nutrients in the pollution. The extra nutrients encourage tiny plants called algae to grow faster than they would normally, forming thick blankets on top of the water. As the blanket of algae begins to rot and die, it removes oxygen from the water. Lack of oxygen kills off other marine life.

WHISTLE BLAST

ROAR OF PROPELLER and SHIP'S ENGINE

Noise is another way to pollute the seas and oceans. Many marine animals, including myself, communicate by sound. Sound waves can carry hundreds of kilometres under water. But it can get a bit noisy down here ...

"WE ALL LIVE IN A YELLOW SUBMARINE

OIL DRILLING

WEAPONS TESTING

Clean water

Now let's turn our backs on the seas and oceans and head inland to look at freshwater and something that we all use every day: clean water. Most people in the developed countries take clean water for granted. It comes out of a tap, it's safe to drink, and it never runs out ... or does it? Even in the UK, with our wet climate, a series of hot, dry summers can cause a water shortage. We need to take more care of this precious resource.

WATER FACTS

• In the developed world, the average person uses between 350 and 1000 litres of water every day. • In the developing world, in areas where there are no taps and people have to rely on water supplies from wells or from rivers, the average person uses as little as five litres every day. • Many people in the developing world are forced to drink dirty water. Dirty water supplies carry diseases such as cholera, typhoid and bilharzia, and cause diarrhoea. • Over 1200 million people do not have access to safe drinking water. • In the developed world, industry uses up vast amounts of water. The manufacture of one car uses about 75,000 litres of water; a tonne of paper uses about 250,000 litres.

PROTECTING ANTARCTICA

The only people in Antarctica are scientists living at the 50 or so research bases, and tourists who visit in cruise ships in the summer months.

In 1991 an 'Environmental Protocol' was drawn up for Antarctica to protect wildlife, and prevent pollution.

In 1961 countries with claims over Antarctica signed an agreement called the Antarctic Treaty. The idea behind the Treaty was that Antarctica should be preserved as a continent for peace and for scientific research.

Atlantic Ocean

70°

80°

A

SOU
Pol

Pacific Ocean

eek - KRILL

There is virtually no wildlife in the centre of Antarctica. But the oceans around Antarctica, and the edge of the continent, are home to huge numbers of seabirds, seals, penguins, whales, and vast amounts of small shrimp-like creatures called krill.

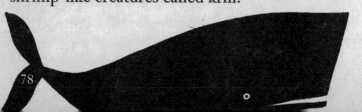

The weather in Antarctica is cold, dry and very windy. Antarctica holds the record for the coldest place (- 89.2°C) and the windiest (322 km per hour).

Antarctica is a huge island, surrounded by oceans and covered by a massive icecap.

Antarctica covers about 12 million square km - that's more than the whole of Europe, or the United States and Mexico combined.

In places the Antarctic icecap is over 4500 metres deep.

Huge icebergs break off the ice into the oceans. The biggest iceberg seen so far was the size of Belgium!

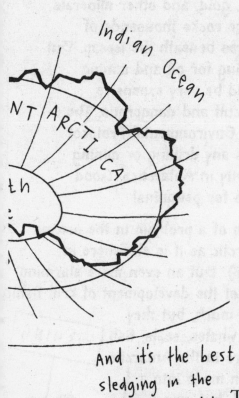

And it's the best sledging in the whole world

The sea freezes around the Antarctic. In summer the area of frozen water is about 2.5 million square km, in winter it extends to about 18 million square km.

Antarctica is the last wilderness on Earth, still relatively unaffected by human influences. What are the main threats to the Antarctic environment?

It's probable that there is oil in Antarctica, not to mention lead, zinc, gold, and other minerals in the rocks thousands of metres beneath the icecap. But drilling for oil and mining would be very expensive, difficult and dangerous. The 1991 Environmental Protocol bans any drilling or mining activity in Antarctica. Good news for penguins!

Overfishing is as much of a problem in the oceans surrounding the Antarctic as it is elsewhere in the world (see page 68). But an even more alarming threat is the prospect of the development of krill fishing. Krill may not look like much, but they are the main food for whales, seals, fish, and seabirds down here in the Antarctic. So far krill hasn't been made into a successful human food, but many countries are still experimenting. If humans fish large quantities of krill will there be enough left to feed the Antarctic wildlife?
Bad news for whales ...

Not many humans live in our part of the world. But they need flat spaces for their airstrips, and they like to be near the sea for their boats to bring supplies during the summer. Unfortunately, these are the places penguins like to live too! And humans make so much rubbish! This is definitely bad news for penguins ...

HUMAN SETTLE-MENT

BOOT

POLLUTION

gasp

One of the main threats comes from the piles of waste created by research bases in the Antarctic. Some of this waste is dumped, some of it is burned. The 1991 Environmental Protocol looks at ways for more of this waste to be removed completely. The environmental balance in the Antarctic is very fragile and any pollution is a serious threat. Pollution is bad news for all Antarctic wildlife ...

Large cruise ships and planes bring tourists to Antarctica. Most tourists are well-behaved but there is always a danger that too many tourists will disrupt wildlife. Ships and planes also create air and water pollution. In the future, it is likely that the numbers of tourists to Antarctica will need to be regulated ...

CLICK

TOURISM

IN THE DODO'S FOOTSTEPS

And now to a subject close to both our hearts – endangered species. All the thousands of animals and plants around the world that are in danger of dying out if something isn't done to help them. We told you the sorry tales of our own extinctions. But what we didn't tell you was that there is a sad second part to the dodo's story. Here it is: the tale of the tambalocque tree.

When I lived on Mauritius I loved nothing better than to sit in the shade of the tambalocque tree. Occasionally a delicious tambalocque fruit would fall to the ground and, using my strong beak, I would crush the seed casing and eat the fruit.

MY WEE DARLIN'

The seeds from the fruit came out in my poo, took root in the ground, and grew into new tambalocque trees.

I was the only bird with a strong enough beak to break open the tambalocque fruit. Ever since I died off in 1681, all those delicious fruits have gone to waste. And even sadder, the tambalocque tree hasn't reproduced for over 300 years ...

OUCH

Scientists estimate that about 100,000 species of animal and plant become extinct every year. (This is only an estimate, as it is very difficult to calculate exact numbers.) But why does it matter?

There are many answers, ranging from 'It matters because every living thing has a right to life, and it shouldn't be up to humans to decide what survives and what doesn't' to 'People will never know how useful an extinct animal or plant might have been.' And, as we saw in the story of the dodo and the tambalocque tree, the extinction of one particular animal or plant can result in the extinction of another - leading to far-reaching and long-term consequences.

Of course, plants and animals were evolving and becoming extinct for millions and millions of years before humans came along. It's a natural process. But humans seem to be doing quite a lot to speed up the process of extinction for many animals and plants.

The place where an animal or plant lives is called a **habitat**. A habitat can be tiny: the community of life forms underneath a stone. Or it can be huge: a whale's habitat is thousands of square kilometres of ocean.

One of the major problems for many endangered creatures is *habitat destruction*. As humans take over more and more of the planet, the natural habitat of many animals and plants is either disappearing completely, or being changed by human influence (for example by air pollution, by DDT poisoning, by oil pollution). One of the most famous animals threatened by habitat destruction is ...

THE GIANT PANDA

Scientific name: *Ailuropoda melanoleuca*
Vital statistics: 1.2-1.5 metres in length; weighs 75-150 kg
Found in: China
Diet: 99% bamboo. An adult panda eats 10-18kg of bamboo every day.
Habitat: Pandas used to be found in a

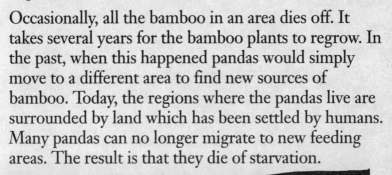

large area of central China. Today, the pandas survive in a few small mountainous areas in the south-west.
Population: In the wild estimated at between 1000 and 2000.

Occasionally, all the bamboo in an area dies off. It takes several years for the bamboo plants to regrow. In the past, when this happened pandas would simply move to a different area to find new sources of bamboo. Today, the regions where the pandas live are surrounded by land which has been settled by humans. Many pandas can no longer migrate to new feeding areas. The result is that they die of starvation.

Conservation solutions

- Protect the areas in which the pandas still live.
- Expand size of existing areas and try to join them into one much bigger region to allow pandas to migrate.
- Involve the local people in any conservation programme. Without their cooperation there is virtually no hope for the survival of the pandas.
- Try to breed pandas in zoos. However, this is extremely difficult, and means that more pandas are removed from the wild.

There is another danger that affects pandas and many other animals - poaching. Many endangered animals are hunted illegally for their skins, or for their horns or their ivory tusks, or to be eaten.

DATING
A GENCY
how to find the
Rhino of your
dreams!

In the 1970s there were about 65,000 black rhino in Africa. Today the number is down to about 2000.

Poachers kill rhino for just one reason: their horns. Rhino horn is used in the North Yemen to make the handles of small daggers worn by Yemeni men. It's also ground up and used in many traditional medicines in Asia. Rhino horns continue to be smuggled out of Africa, and to fetch large amounts of money on the black market.

Desperate measures are needed to save the few remaining black rhino. The import of rhino horn is now banned in North Yemen. Alternatives to rhino horn are being promoted for use in traditional medicines. In Namibia, the situation got so serious that scientists decide to remove rhinos' horns themselves to make the animals worthless to poachers. In other parts of Africa, rhinos are kept in fenced-off reserves with round-the-clock armed guards. Only by ending the demand for rhino horn can poaching be stopped. Promoting wildlife tourism, so that a live rhino is worth more than a dead one, is also a solution.

Why don't we just round up all the humans and put them in a fenced-off reserve with a round-the-clock guard? That should do it!

Human actions other than poaching pose threats to animals. First, as humans have spread around the world, they have taken plants and animals with them. This often has a damaging effect on the local wildlife. For example, goats were taken to the island of St Helena in the South Atlantic in 1513. Goats eat everything, so since then, many of the plant species on the island have become extinct. Secondly, the legal and illegal markets for exotic plants and animals continue to flourish. Parrots, tortoises, tropical fish are captured and exported to be sold for pets. Cacti and orchids are dug up from the wild to be cultivated in gardens.

87

What about us?

Many of the plants and animals on the endangered list aren't particularly cuddly or attractive, but they all have their own story, and they are just as important as the panda, or the rhino, or the elephant, the tiger, the leopard, the whales ...

Hello, I'm a coelacanth. I live along the East African coast. No one really knew about me until 1938 when a fishermen caught a coelacanth. There was a great hoo-ha and museums all over the world suddenly wanted coela-canths for their precious collections – it was terrible!

I'm a freshwater pearly mussel. As you can see I'm very beautiful, and I make exquisite pearls which humans seem to get very excited about. So excited that I'm struggling to survive, what with the pearl fishermen and the pollution! Ugh!

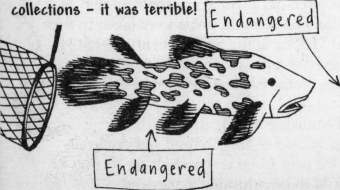

Endangered

Endangered

Conservation efforts

- **Reserves and parks** aim to protect both habitat and wildlife in a specific area. But it's very important to involve local people and listen to their views too. And protecting wildlife costs money which many developing countries can ill-afford.
- **Laws** to ban hunting and trade are often drawn up as international treaties. One of the best-known is CITES (the Convention on International Trade in Endangered Species of Wild Fauna and Flora) which controls the trade of endangered species. However, treaties will only work if countries are prepared to enforce laws, and this again costs money.
- **Zoos** are the last resort. If animals cannot be protected in the wild, efforts are often made to breed them in captivity.

eah, well I'm the LARGEST arwig in the world and I live n St Helena. Some fool rought some goats over here nd since then my habitat has hanged somewhat. Oh, and I orgot to mention the mice and entipedes, also introduced, ho seem to like me for their upper. This is no fun!

I'm a Houston toad. I live in Texas, USA. My habitat is disappearing under tarmac and houses. And I don't like the change in climate which seems to be getting hotter and drier. Are you humans responsible for that too?

Stamp

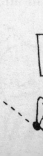

Endangered

Endangered

89

FEEDING THE PEOPLE

In 1994, roughly 94 million new babies were born: approximately 5 million to families in the developed world, but approximately 89 million to families in the developing world.

In 1997, the population in Africa is about 720 million, but by 2025, it is estimated that the population of Africa will be about 1510 million. In comparison, the population of Europe in 1997 is about 729 million, but by 2025, it is estimated that the population of Europe will be about 743 million.

Rattle

why do you never see baby passenger pigeons?

Why are people in the developing world having more children than people in the developed world? As usual, there isn't one simple answer, there are several complicated ones:

1. Lack of access to family planning. Many women in developing countries have few rights, and little choice about the number of children they have.

2. Children play an active part in earning money for the household, and in supporting their parents. In countries where there are no pensions, and people have no opportunity to save money, this is very important. Children are a kind of insurance.

3. Large families are a status symbol in many countries.

4. People love children!

Some people see **overpopulation** as the root cause of many ills. Overpopulation is used as an explanation for shortages of food and famine.

"Too many people – not enough food to go round."

Overpopulation is also used to explain environmental problems such as soil erosion and **desertification**. This happens when humans strip the resources of an area by over use so that the land becomes barren desert. This usually happens on the fringes of existing deserts.

But hold on! This all sounds suspiciously simple to me. Let's look a bit closer at the major causes of famine, desertification and soil erosion.

QUIZ
Why do people die of starvation?

1. There just isn't enough food to go round.
2. Food is available, but people can't afford to buy it.
3. The supermarket shut early.

Research suggests that number 2 is the most common cause - poor people are too poor to buy food, even though it is available. So the problem isn't that there isn't enough food, the problem is the way it's shared out.

People in the developed countries eat on average 30-40% more calories than they need. Many people in the developing countries get 10% less than the basic minimum, and as this is an average figure many people exist on even less than this.

Every day, across the world, about 800 million poor people face hunger. But the only times when most people in the developed world realise that others are starving is during FAMINES.

In the 1980s, famine in Africa hit the headlines. A severe drought led to the failure of crops, and in 1984-5 nearly one million people died from starvation. If the crops failed in the UK or USA, the government would buy extra food from abroad to make up the shortfall. The food would be more expensive, but most people would have enough money to afford it. There would be no famine. So why did people in Africa starve to death during the famines of the 1980s?

Dinkanesh has a small plot of land where he grows enough food to feed his family. Some years there is a small amount of surplus food that he sells at the local market.

Recently, though, things have been bad. The rains haven't come, and Dinkanesh is struggling to produce enough food for his family. His wife is extra careful with the food they do have, and tries to make it go as far as possible. She feeds the children first; she and Dinkanesh often go hungry.

The crops have failed. There is food to buy at the local market, so Dinkanesh starts to sell some of the household possessions, tools, some pots and pans. They buy supplies, but soon the supplies run out. He decides to look for a job.

Many other poor farmers have had the same idea. There are too many people looking for too few jobs on large farms, and in the cities. The wages are getting lower every day, and the price of food is getting higher ...

Like Dinkanesh, most of the world's poor people live in rural areas and rely on what they can grow to survive. This is called **subsistence farming**.

But governments in developing countries are often more interested in crops that can be exported and sold overseas, such as cotton, tea, coffee, cocoa, bananas, sugar, tobacco, rubber, peanuts etc. These crops are known as **cash crops**. (Instead of being grown for the local people to eat, they are grown in order to be sold for money.)

Cash crops:

- take away land from local subsistence farmers

- often push subsistence farmers onto poorer land

- are often grown on large, modern farms which use up large amounts of water for irrigation, as well as fertilizers and pesticides

- are also grown on a much smaller scale by poor farmers in addition to their subsistence crops

Even during the famine of 1984-5, Ethiopia continued to export its cash crops to earn much-needed money abroad.

With the introduction of modern, large-scale farming methods, the traditional ways of farming are losing out. But does this matter? After all, modern farming methods are better aren't they?

In the past, many 'experts' (often from the West) dismissed traditional methods of farming in Africa as backward and old-fashioned. But recently there has been a rethink, as people have begun to realise the value of these farming methods. For instance, many African farmers traditionally practised shifting cultivation, like the rainforest peoples. By using a plot for only a year or two before abandoning it and moving elsewhere, they allowed the soil to recover its fertility.

Think of a field and you probably see a large area full of the same plant: wheat, or barley, or corn. But in Africa, small farmers are much more likely to grow a variety of different plants on their plots of land. This is called **mixed cropping**.

Mixed cropping has many advantages:
- The plot is fully covered with plants. (For instance, a tree crop such as bananas, with a grain crop beneath it, and at ground-level, beans or peas.) This means less weeding!
- The tall plants provide shelter for the smaller ones. Some of the plants also produce natural fertilisers which help the other plants to grow.
- The plants are less likely to get diseases than if there was just one single crop.
- If one crop fails the farmer still has the other plants to fall back on.
- The crops don't all ripen at the same time.
- The farmer gets a supply of different foods.
- Such close planting prevents soil erosion.
- As well as growing food for eating, the farmer can grow a cash crop to sell at market.

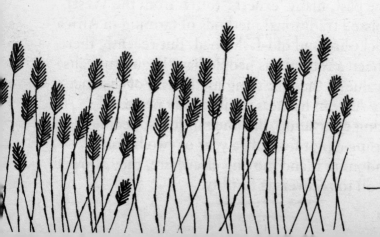

The problem for poor farmers in Africa and elsewhere is that they have been pushed on to poorer, less-fertile land. They are forced to over-exploit the land simply to survive.

This soil is exhausted and infertile, but there is nowhere else for me to go to try to grow my crops ...

We used to cut only dead wood from the trees for fuelwood. But now nearly all the trees have gone ... What can we do? We need fuelwood for cooking.

I can remember coming here to graze my cattle. But they cleared us out to grow sorghum here. Now the topsoil has blown away, and the place is a desert.

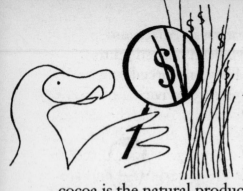

Finally, let's have a closer look at cash crops ...

Most developing countries earn most of their foreign cash by exporting natural products. For instance, cocoa is the natural product used to make chocolate, cotton is the natural product used to make many clothes, sugar is a natural product found in all sorts of foods and drinks. These natural products are often called **commodities**. The trouble is that the prices of these commodities are decided not by the producers, but by financial dealers in London, New York, Frankfurt, Tokyo ...

So if the price of a commodity goes down, the amount earned by the exporting country goes down too. For instance, in 1989, the price of coffee on the world markets dropped suddenly. Farmers in Uganda left coffee beans rotting on the bushes because the price was so low it was not worth picking them.

Many developing countries would like to stop being so dependent on exporting commodities, and develop trade in manufactured goods instead. (For instance, instead of exporting cocoa, they could export the manufactured product chocolate. Instead of exporting cotton, they could export clothes.) You can charge more for manufactured goods, so they earn more for the exporter, and are not so vulnerable to price changes. But most developed countries impose limits and barriers to the number of manufactured goods being imported from the developing world. They claim that they do this to protect jobs in their own manufacturing industries.

If they produce clothes cheaper than we can, people will want to buy their clothes instead of ours, so we'll be out of work!

It may seem as if we've come away from the subject of this book. But throughout this section, you will have noticed that most environmental issues seem to come back to the question of money. The governments and the people of the poorer countries are forced into situations about which they have little choice. For them, in their fight for day-to-day survival, concern for the environment is often a luxury that they simply cannot afford.

FIGHTING THE WAR

One of the things which all the African countries that experienced famine in the 1980s had in common was **civil war**. War in any form is a disaster not only for the people caught up in it, but also for the environment. It affects everyone and everything.

Sometimes natural resources are deliberately destroyed or polluted by one side in a war. During the Gulf War, Iraqi troops set fire to oil wells in Kuwait, causing vast amounts of air pollution and wasting millions of gallons of oil. A large amount of oil also polluted the Kuwait coastline, killing over 30,000 sea birds.

War disrupts the economic life of a country.

War often forces people to leave their homes, their crops, their animals and to become refugees. Huge numbers of refugees can strain the resources of a 'safe' area to the limit. In order to survive, refugees often have few choices.

Habitat destruction is a serious outcome of war. It was a problem even during the reign of Henry VIII when many of England's oak trees were cut down to make warships.

Vegetation and crops are often deliberately destroyed. For instance, as part of their war tactics in the Vietnamese War, the US army sprayed herbicide (chemicals that kill vegetation) over a vast area of Vietnam. This spraying destroyed tropical forests, and about half of the mangrove forests in the Mekong Delta. The long-term effects are still being assessed today.

During times of war, wildlife is often seriously endangered. People may be forced to hunt 'protected' animals for food. This happened in Uganda, when people killed huge numbers of elephants and rhinos in order to avoid starvation.

Even after a war has finished, the effects continue to be felt. Landmines can take years to clear. They cause injury or death to animals and people alike.

The last point about war is that it is expensive! More money is spent on weapons and armies instead of on developing industry or on health care and education.

101

Ironically the **environment** itself can often be a cause of conflict. People have long gone to war over patches of land ...

It's mine!

No, it's mine!

... over raw materials ...

It's mine!

No, it's mine!

... over water supplies ...

It's mine!

No, it's mine!

... even over fish! In the 1970s Britain and Iceland waged a war without weapons over their rights to fish the North Sea. It was called the 'cod war'!

and guess who the casualties were?

In 1945, the USA dropped two nuclear bombs on Hiroshima and Nagasaki in Japan. The explosions killed about 190,000 people. Since then no nuclear weapons have been used in warfare. However, many countries hold nuclear weapons to deter other countries from attacking them.

What would happen if a nuclear war did break out? One possible scenario put forward by scientists goes like this:

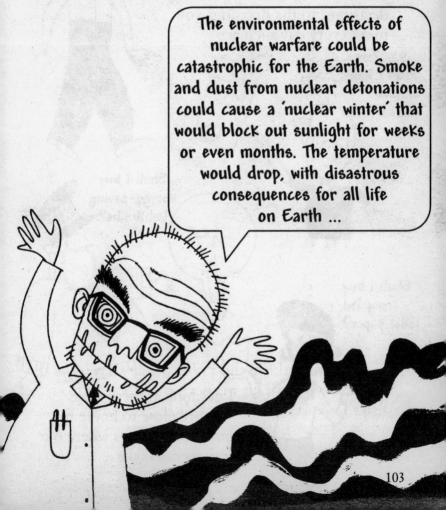

The environmental effects of nuclear warfare could be catastrophic for the Earth. Smoke and dust from nuclear detonations could cause a 'nuclear winter' that would block out sunlight for weeks or even months. The temperature would drop, with disastrous consequences for all life on Earth ...

Planning a greener future

If we are going to try to tackle the major issues outlined in this book, people at every level need to do something about environmental concerns, from international conferences, to the laws by governments, to local planning decisions, to the decisions you make every day such as:

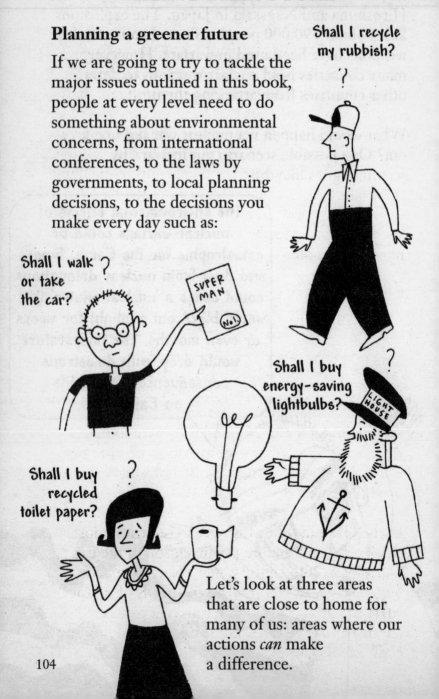

Shall I recycle my rubbish?

Shall I walk or take the car?

SUPER MAN No.1

Shall I buy energy-saving lightbulbs?

LIGHT HOUSE

Shall I buy recycled toilet paper?

Let's look at three areas that are close to home for many of us: areas where our actions *can* make a difference.

104

1 TRANSPORT

In 1965 the average person in Western Europe drove 8 km per day. By 1995, the figure had gone up to 25 km per day. We all know that burning fossil fuels is bad news for the environment, and that we should use our cars less, but cars are comfortable and convenient - it's difficult to give them up. This is mostly a problem of the developed world where car ownership is on a huge scale compared to most countries of the developing world. In the USA there are 730 cars for every 1000 people: in India the figure is 6 cars per 1000 people.

I love my car!

ROAR

ZOOM

So why do people in the USA have so many cars? It's partly that it's difficult to go anywhere without a car! Many urban areas have been planned with the car in mind. Schools and shops are too far from houses for anyone to walk between the two. Petrol is cheap, and many households have two or even three cars.

In the UK and other European countries, most cities were built before the invention of the car. During the 20th century, new roads have been built to try to accommodate the needs of motor vehicles. Often the result has been a concrete jungle where the car is king and people definitely come second best!

What are the alternatives to the car?

Walking! How many short journeys per week do you make by car that you could walk instead?

Cycling! This is becoming more and more popular, but safety is a problem. More could be done on the roads with cycle lanes and special cycle tracks to make cycling safer and even more appealing.

Public transport! Travel by train or coach is more environmentally friendly than using your car, but often less convenient and sometimes more expensive. How can people be encouraged to use public transport more? This is a particularly important question in cities, where streets are often gridlocked because of too many cars.

Curitiba is a city in Brazil. Over the last 20 years it has developed an integrated public transport system. This means that Curitiba has lots of buses that run regularly, connect with each other, and are cheap to use. There are fast express buses, and smaller local buses. You can buy one ticket to use on any bus. The buses run on special bus lanes, so that they don't get stuck in traffic jams. The buses have cut the amount of fuel used by vehicles in the city by about a quarter: this is more efficient and causes less pollution. The government planned housing and bus routes together, developing land along the routes into new houses for poorer families. Over 1.3 million people ride on Curitiba's buses every day. A success story!

Finally, it would be a good idea to improve the cars we do use: spending more money on fuel-efficiency, clean-burn engines, technology for clean electric cars, and alternative fuels such as hydrogen, methanol and ethanol - instead of investing money on making cars look sexy!

2 AT HOME

There are lots of ways that you can help the environment at home and there are lots of books around that tell you what to do! Look in the reading list on pages 118-119 if you want to find out more.

Shopping

Take one bar of plain chocolate costing £1.
Who gets what?

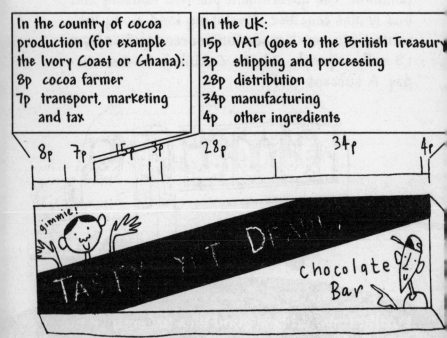

In the country of cocoa production (for example the Ivory Coast or Ghana):
8p cocoa farmer
7p transport, marketing and tax

In the UK:
15p VAT (goes to the British Treasury
3p shipping and processing
28p distribution
34p manufacturing
4p other ingredients

8p 7p 15p 3p 28p 34p 4p

gimmie!

TASTY YIT DEADLY

chocolate Bar

(Figures from the World Development Movement)

For every bar of £1 chocolate sold, the British government gets more than twice as much in tax (VAT) than the farmer who grows the cocoa beans.

However, you can help farmers in developing countries by buying goods that are sold under the *Fairtrade* scheme. Look for this symbol:

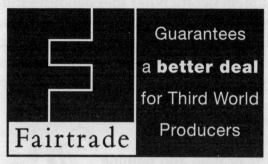

Guarantees a **better deal** for Third World Producers

Fairtrade

The Fairtrade scheme ensures that the farmer is paid a fair amount for his or her products. It also guarantees fundamental human rights to decent wages, worker representation, security and minimum health and safety standards.

You can also help the environment by buying locally produced food. Next time you are in your local superstore have a look at where the food comes from - particularly the fresh fruits and vegetables. Transporting food across the globe uses up vast amounts of fossil fuels and causes air pollution. Think 'green' (see page 17)! Visit your local greengrocer or farm shop and buy local fruit and veg (preferably **organic**, which means grown without using artificial fertilizers or pesticides).

Ach.
It's turnips
for dinner
again –
tonight

Building for the future

What about making buildings themselves more environmentally friendly? Old buildings can be improved, and planning for new buildings needs to take environmental concerns into account at the earliest stages. Let's look at a 'green' house to see how it is designed to help the environment.

Energy efficiency! Cut down on the amount of energy used for heating and lighting by insulation, double glazing, etc.

Solar energy! Use energy from the sun rather than burning fossil fuels to provide energy for heat, light, cooking etc.

Conserving water! 32% of the water used in the average house in the UK goes down the toilet! In the 'green' house, rainwater could be collected and filtered to provide enough for household use.

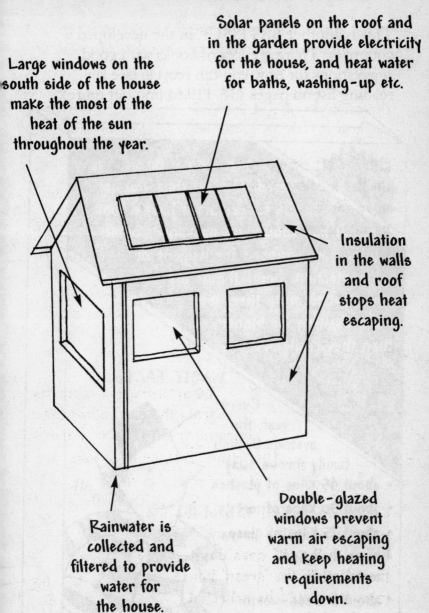

Solar panels on the roof and in the garden provide electricity for the house, and heat water for baths, washing-up etc.

Large windows on the south side of the house make the most of the heat of the sun throughout the year.

Insulation in the walls and roof stops heat escaping.

Rainwater is collected and filtered to provide water for the house.

Double-glazed windows prevent warm air escaping and keep heating requirements down.

This is another BIG ISSUE in the developed
countries. There are lots of books with good
suggestions for how you can recycle (see the
reading list on pages 118-119 to find out more).

Packaging – do we
need it? Next time you go
to the supermarket have a look
at how things are packaged. Some
things are wrapped for hygiene or
for protection. Some things are
packaged to make them look
more exciting, or bigger
than they really are.

WASTE FACTS

Every
year, the
average British
family throws away:

- about 45 kilos of plastics
- about 30 kilos of metals
- about 75 kilos of glass
- more than 500
  metal cans
- about 6 trees-worth
  of paper.

WINK

Our main effort should be to reduce the amount of waste we produce in the first place. But what can be reused or recycled?

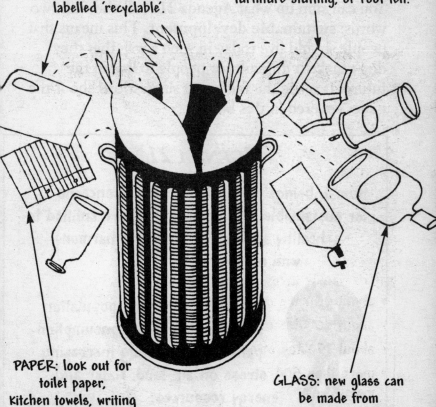

PLASTICS: are complicated. Many products are made from different kinds of plastics, and are difficult to recycle. Plastics which can be recycled are usually labelled 'recyclable'.

TEXTILES: don't throw away old clothes! If they are in good condition take them to a charity shop, or put them in a textile bank so that they can be rewoven, or used to make furniture stuffing, or roof felt.

PAPER: look out for toilet paper, kitchen towels, writing paper and exercise books made from recycled paper.

GLASS: new glass can be made from smashed-up old bottles, called cullet.

Besides all these things that we can do as individuals, governments are also committed to looking after the environment. In June 1992, they agreed 'an action plan for the 1990s and well into the 21st century' at a United Nations Conference called the Earth Summit, in Rio de Janeiro, Brazil. This action plan, known as Agenda 21 was signed by 179 nations who all agreed to the aims of its 40 chapters.

You can sum up what Agenda 21 is all about in two words: **sustainable development**. This means that people should live today in such a way that they don't make it difficult for people to live in the future. It made the following suggestions about the issues covered in this book:

AGENDA 21

Human beings are at the centre of concerns for sustainable development. They are entitled to healthy and productive life in harmony with nature.

The world's growing population and unsustainable consumption patterns are putting increasing stress on air, land, water and energy resources.

Hungry + Homeless

Governments must get greater energy efficiency out of existing power stations and develop new, renewable energy sources such as solar, wind, hydro, ocean and human power.

Oceans are under increasing stress from pollution, overfishing and general degradation. It affects everything from the climate to coral reefs.

All social and economic activity relies heavily on fresh water. Water is becoming scarce in many countries. The management of water resources is of paramount importance in the 1990s and beyond.

The root causes of poverty are hunger, illiteracy, inadequate medical care, unemployment and population pressures.

Poverty is a major factor in soil degradation. We need to restore fragile lands and find new jobs for farmers thrown out of work.

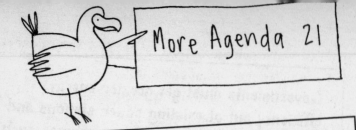

The major cause of the continued deterioration of the global environment is the unsustainable pattern of consumption and production, particularly in the industrialized countries.

Developed countries should take the lead in achieving sustainable consumption patterns ...

The development process will not gain momentum if the developing countries are weighed down by external indebtedness, if development finance is inadequate, if barriers restrict access to markets and if commodity prices and the terms of trade of developing countries remain depressed.

While managing resources sustainably, an environmental policy that focuses mainly on conservation and protection of resources must take due account of those who depend on the resources for their livelihoods.

must consume
useless junk —

Urgent and decisive action is needed to conserve and maintain genes, species and ecosystems, with a view to sustainable management and the use of biological resources.

Warfare is inherently destructive of sustainable development.

All energy sources will need to be used in ways that respect the atmosphere, human health and the environment as a whole.

By the year 2025, 83 % of the expected global population of 8.5 billion will be living in developing countries.

More than half the world's population lives within 60 km of the shoreline, and this could rise to three quarters by the year 2020. Many of the world's poor are crowded in coastal areas. Coastal resources are vital for many local communities ...

And finally, for children in all countries of the world:

The involvement of today's youth in environment and development decision-making and in the implementation of programmes is critical to the long-term success of Agenda 21.

THIS MEANS THAT IT'S UP TO YOU!

What to do next...

OK. You've read the book, NOW what do you do?

There are lots and lots of other books about the environment. Some will tell you about how to use energy more efficiently, how to recycle, how to be a thorough 'greenie'! Some concentrate on conservation issues, others take a wide-ranging look at environmental problems. Here are a few you might like to look up at your local library or bookshop:

The Young Green Consumer Guide by John Elkington and Julia Hailes (Guild Publishing)
The Young Person's Guide to the Environment (Practical Ways of Making a Difference) by John Howson (Souvenir Press)
The WWF Environment Handbook by Mark Carwardine (Optima)
Rescue Mission Planet Earth (A Children's edition of Agenda 21) by children of the world (Kingfisher Books)
Captain Eco and the Fate of the Earth by Jonathon Porritt and Ellis Nadler
Ecology for Beginners by Stephen Croall and William Rankin (Icon)
Usborne Science and Experiments: Ecology by Richard Spurgeon (Usborne)
Understanding Global issues Editor: Richard Buckley. A series obtainable from European Schoolbooks Publishing Ltd, The Runnings, Cheltenham, GL51 9PQ. Titles include: *The Battle for Water; World Population; World Fishing; Renewable Energy; Antarctica.*

In your local library there should be an environment section in the reference section. This has books that you probably wouldn't want to buy, or read from beginning to end, but which are useful for looking things up:

Green Pages – A Directory of Natural Products, Services, Resources and Ideas compiled by John Button (Optima)

Green Globe Yearbook of International Co-operation on Environment and Development The Fridtjof Nansen Institute. (This is a handbook of international action on the environment.)

The Earth Report 3 – An A-Z Guide to Environmental Issues Editors: Edward Goldsmith and Nicholas Hildyard

Who's Who in the Environment The Environment Council. (Separate publications for England and Scotland. Lists environmental organisations.)

Agenda 21 – The UN Action Programme from Rio.

Sustainable Development: The UK Strategy HMSO. (A publication about the UK arising out of the Earth Summit.)

You don't happen to know any bees do you?

what's the big idea?!

You could join a local environmental organisation. Or you could contact one of the nationwide organisations that campaign about environmental and related issues, such as:

Fairtrade Foundation
7th floor, Regent House
89 Kingsway
London WC2B 6RH
0171 405 5942

Friends of the Earth
26-28 Underwood Street
London N1 7JQ
0171 490 1555

Gaia Foundation
18 Well Walk
London NW3 1LD
0171 435 5000
Highlights the importance of ecological and cultural diversity.

Greennet
Bradley Close
74-77 White Lion St
London N1 9PF
0171713 1941
e-mail address: support@gn.apc.org

Greenpeace
Canonbury Villas
London N1 2PN
0171 865 8100

Intermediate Technology
Myson House
Railway terrace
Rugby
Warwickshire CV21 3HT
01788 560631
IT works to enable poor people in the developing
countries to develop and use technologies which
contribute towards sustainable development.

Oxfam
274 Banbury Road
Oxford OX2 7DZ
01865 311311

Population Concern
178-202 Great Portland Street
London W1N 5TB
0171 631 1546

Rescue Mission Headquarters
Peace Child International Centre
The White House
Buntingford
Herts SG9 9AH
01763 274459

Royal Society for the Protection of Birds
The Lodge
Sandy
Bedfordshire SG19 2DL
01767 680551

Surfers against Sewage
The Old Counthouse Warehouse
Wheal Kitty
St Agnes
Cornwall TR5 0RE
01872 553001

Survival International
11-15 Emerald Street
London WC1N 3QL
0171 242 1441

Sustrans
35 King Street
Bristol BS1 4DZ
0117 926 8893
Plans, builds and maintains
safe non-motor routes.

Transport 2000
Walkden House
10 Melton Street
London NW1 2EJ
0171 388 8386
Aims to promote
environmentally
sound transport policies.

Waste Watch
Gresham House
24 Holborn Viaduct
London EC1A 2BN
0171 248 1818

Whale and Dolphin Conservation Society
Alexander House
James Street West
Bath BA1 2BT
01225 334511

World Development Movement
25 Beehive Place
London SW9 7QR
0171 737 6215

World Wide Fund for Nature
Panda House
Weyside Park
Godalming
Surrey GU7 1XR
01483 426444

Young People's Trust for the Environment and
Nature Conservation
8 Leapale Road
Guildford
Surrey GU1 4JX
01483 39600

glossary

acid rain rain that is made more acid than normal as a result of pollution in the air.

biomass plant material used as a source of energy.

carbon a chemical element found in different forms in all living things.

cash crop crops grown to be sold for money, often for export.

chlorofluorocarbon (CFC) a molecule made from chlorine, fluoride and carbon atoms. The breakdown of CFCs in the atmosphere destroys ozone in the ozone layer.

commodities natural products or raw materials such as tea, coffee and rubber which are sold on the world market.

deforestation the clearance of trees by cutting or burning.

desertification the process by which the resources of an area of land become so overstretched by human use that the land becomes a barren desert.

developed countries countries with developed industries and a generally high standard of living.

developing countries countries with less developed industry and a generally low standard of living.

ecology the study of the relationships between living things and their environment.

ecosystem the web of connections linking all the animals and plants in a particular environment.

erosion the wearing away of soil or rocks by wind, water or ice.

extinct an animal or plant becomes extinct when the last of its species dies out.

fossil fuels coal, oil and natural gas. These fuels are formed over millions of years from the remains of animals and plants.

geothermal power energy taken from hot rocks beneath the surface of the Earth.

greenhouse gases the gases trapped within Earth's atmosphere that help to keep the temperature of the Earth stable. They are carbon dioxide, methane, water vapour and nitrous oxide. Human activity has increased the amount of greenhouse gases in the Earth's atmosphere. This is known as the greenhouse effect.

habitat the environment in which a plant or an animal lives.

hydropower energy from falling or moving water.

mixed cropping the system of growing different crops together in the same plot.

non-renewable fuels fuels such as coal, oil and gas which will eventually run out.

nuclear fission the process of splitting an atom. As the atom splits it releases nuclear energy.

organic a plant that has been grown organically has been grown without the use of any chemical pesticides or fertilizers.

ozone a gas made from three oxygen atoms. Most ozone lies in a layer in the Earth's atmosphere between about 10 and 50 kilometres above your head.

pesticides chemicals used to kill insects that attack crops.

photosynthesis the process by which plants use energy from the sun, water and carbon dioxide to make food.

rainforest moist, hot forest regions that lie in the tropics.

recycling the process of using something again rather than throwing it away.

renewable energy energy made from sources that cannot be used up, for example solar energy.

shifting cultivation a system of farming in which small areas of land are cleared and farmed for a short time before being left to grow back. This type of farming ensures that the land does not become exhausted and infertile.

subsistence farming subsistence farmers rely on what they can grow to survive. There is often little or nothing left over as surplus for sale.

sustainable development the principle that people should live today in such a way that they don't make it difficult for people to live in the future.

food for thought is all very well but give me a tin of cat food any day.

INDEX